First Truth

poems
Bertha Wise

Clare Songbirds Publishing House Poetry Series
ISBN 978-1-947653-89-4
Clare Songbirds Publishing House
First Truth © 2020 Bertha Wise

All Rights Reserved. Permission to reprint individual poems must be obtained from the author who owns the copyright.

Printed in the United States of America
FIRST EDITION

Original cover photo © 2020 Donna J. Ward

Clare Songbirds Publishing House Mission Statement:
Clare Songbirds Publishing House was established to provide a print forum for the creation of limited edition, fine art from poets and writers, both established and emerging. We strive to reignite and continue a tradition of quality, accessible literary arts to the national and international community of writers, and readers. Chapbook manuscripts are carefully chosen for their ability to propel the expansion of art and ideas in literary form. We provide an accessible way to promote the art of words in order to resonate with, and impact, readers not yet familiar with the siren song of poets and writers. Clare Songbirds Publishing House espouses a singular cultural development where poetry creates community and becomes commonplace in public places.

140 Cottage Street
Auburn, New York 13021
www.claresongbirdspub.com

Contents

Turns	7
Truth in a Dipper	8
Tea Time	9
Firsts	10
Grandpa's Wisdom	12
Crooked Time	13
Old Sayings	14
Constant Velocity	15
Breaking Things	16
Berry Picking	17
Pressing Down Hard	18
Magic	20
Dandelions	21
Spring Faith	22
Sunrise	23
Transition	24
Overturned Life	25
Mourning Dove	26
How It Is	27
Autumn Colors	28
Autumn Meditation	29
Eclipse	30
Taking Flight	31
Prayer	32
Snow Falling	33
Hope– Preface	34
Hope	35
Armistice, 1918	36
Motorbiking in Wales	37
One Evening in Budapest	38
Finding Shoes	40
Moonlight Sonata	41
Your World	42
Making the Grade	43
Joy of Giving	45

Acknowledgments

"Truth in a Dipper", Redbud (anthology at OSU-OKC), 1988
"Pressing Down Hard", Absolute (anthology at Oklahoma City Community College, 2001
"Making the Grade", Absolute, 2004

"One Evening in Budapest", Absolute, 2005

"Breaking Things", Absolute, 2006

"Finding Shoes" (under the title "Finding the Right Pair of Shoes"), Absolute, 2009

"Overturned Life", Dragon Poet Review, 2016

With appreciation to family, friends, colleagues and all the poets I've read and loved in my life, I dedicate these poems.

My husband Guy deserves a special note of gratitude for being willing to eat a frozen dinner or takeout so I could work on this book.

Friends and colleagues through the years deserve recognition too, but I cannot list them all for fear of omitting someone who could haunt me. Suffice it say, their encouragement to write and willingness to read or listen to my words spurred me to continue even when I had other things to do. It's their fault if my house is a mess sometimes.

Finally, I have to give my mom, dad, grandmother, sisters, brother and cousin their due because they so often pop up in my poetry with sweet memories.

Turns

Ya know how ya can go along
La-la-la—
asking anyone ya meet
How's it going? How're ya doin'?

Fine.
Okay.
Glad it's Friday!
all the usual answers
come flying back—

Then—
you take a sharp right turn
and run into someone
who stops short
eyes filling—not smiling
and the words come rushing out
"My best friend is dying
And I'm going to miss him so much!"

All you can do is stand there
silent for a moment
trying to gather the courage
to hug the person
and promise things will be okay—

Ya just have to keep going along
La-la-la—
asking everyone ya meet
How's it going? How're ya doin'?
waiting for the turns.

Truth in a Dipper

Seeing the Big Dipper
on an invisible hook
hanging on the black wall of sky,
I wonder what Truth
is told among the stars.

Summer Sundays at Grandma's
found us playing
"Stone school"
"Mother may I?"
"Gossip"—
imitating adults
where truth became
distorted with re-telling it
like cicadas chattering.

We got hot and thirsty
for the cool, crystal
spring-drawn liquid
kept in its bucket
in the dim woodshed.

Sipping
from the enameled dipper,
we tasted truth
in its purest form
and It
quenched our thirst.

Tea Time

At this time of day
when light grows thin
and time for a cup of tea
I think of you—
of your gentle ways
your quiet wisdom
as you stir the spoon
to cool the tea
just enough—

you teach me how to drink it
with a bit of milk
just enough—

you show me how
to hold the china cup
like a lady—
noiseless
without flourish—

it's that time of day
when a grandmother
passes on something special
just enough.

Firsts

There's a first time for everything
I'm told
and I remember many firsts
such as
the first day in kindergarten when I cried
not to be left there without my mother's smell
but the teacher smelled like lilacs which was
the first time I'd smelled them on someone so
after that I made it to first grade and moved on
without my mother

all the way to the seventh grade at
a new school in a new town in a different state
where foreign southern rules confused me and
on the first day I missed the right bus and
on the way home to find my mother I peed my pants and cried
sure that I was lost until the driver handed me off to
an unknown neighbor who delivered me to my
mother and I noticed her worried eyes for the first time
as though she knew I would get lost again
but I didn't yet.

My first kiss at age fourteen came from a boy
whose first kiss was me after
we walked home from our first dance
arousing first sensations of heat rising
in the cool darkness at my back door
where in the shadows we embraced
our lips brushing then opening to the first kiss
of love, or what passed for it through the summer,
and into our first year of high school toward separate destinies.

Moving away brought rapid firsts in succession:
puffing a cigarette that ended my career as a smoker
hot nights at the drive-in and first practicing
sex with a lucky guy who first showed me the
power that I held with fear but excitement at the same time
the first heartbreak came too with the same lucky guy
because I wouldn't go all the way with him for the first time
on my birthday and he blamed me for his quitting school

which was my first guilt trip.

After high school graduation I finally did have my first
real sex but didn't think it was much until
I met my first love that I loved for more than sex

which scared him silly so he introduced me to a friend
who became my first husband with whom
I had a first baby that died right after being born
far away from home for the first time
where my mother couldn't hold me
and help me mourn over my first loss.

Years later we finally cried together
she and I
in an anti-climactic first that made me
know that she'd had her firsts too.

I reached adulthood for the first time.

Grandpa's Wisdom

Grandpa always said,
"Look out for him!
He's slicker than owl shit!"

and the
local silver-tongued
Romeo who tried to get
into every girl's drawers.

Grandpa would sit back
in his rocker,
draw on his pipe
and exhale wisdom
for my benefit
in hopes that I would
never be seduced
by anyone whose
charming ways and
quick wits spun magic.

He knew the ways
of the heart
could be treacherous.

He knew words
that floated like smoke,
obscured real motives
and created
false trust—
because

he had once been
that Romeo who had made
the rounds, left behind
broken promises
and girls
with nothing to show for
what they'd been
talked out of.

Yes, Grandpa always said,
"Look out for him!
He's slicker than owl shit!"

Crooked Time

I have lived in crooked time
I've been awakened at
2:57 a.m.
in Florida
where I'm teaching
an e. e. cummings poem
to present students
to former students
AND
H O R R O R S!
to a former professor from Oklahoma
who hates e.e. cummings
AND
the poem is nonexistent.

I have lived in straight time
I've awakened at
6:30 a.m.
where I knew
next week next month
next year
high school graduation
marriage
babies
Disney World
divorce
death.

I prefer crooked time.

Old Sayings

My folks always had a large garden
started in May when danger of frost
was past and spring eased into summer.
Sweet corn was a staple
grown year to year—
my dad said the corn
had to be knee-high
by Fourth of July—
an old saying he knew—
but backbreaking work with plow
cultivator, hoe and planter came first—
my father rummaged
to find the old planter
a one-footed gadget
with a hopper holding corn seed
dispensed one at a time
as he pressed the planter
causing the spring to
release a kernel
into the tilled ground.
Behind him, I followed
to cover each seed
out of sight of the sun
hoping the crop
would grow.
In June
we saw green sprouts
grow into stalks by
the Fourth of July.
By the end of the month,
the stalks had skinny ears
that grew white silky tassels.
By August
fat yellow ears bulged in their husks
with dark brown topknots—
ready to pull.
We'd have
sweet, buttered
corn on the cob
because old sayings
came true.

Constant Velocity

My grandmother
believed in constant velocity
even though she would not have
known what it was.
Silently
the ruins of the old canal
waited just across the road
from my grandmother's house
as if time would take
care of the stones
stacked
on top of stones,
but they slowly
returned to the earth
until I could only see
a faint outline
of a time gone by.
At grandmother's,
time passed
with the whisper
of a ticking kitchen clock
as it measured out the seconds
and the minutes
into cupfuls
of sugar and flour and milk
mixed with yeast to make It
rise just in time
to bake bread
in the Ever-Ready oven,
warmth adding to the
quiet drowsiness as if
the red poppies in her garden
had invaded the house
and made me want
to sleep
in peaceful slumber
never to awaken
from the swirl of Time
afraid that It would
carry me along too fast
into the future
and the past.

Breaking Things

breaking things—
an arm by accident
toys in play
an alarm clock from curiosity
pencils from pressing down too hard

breaking things—
the first heart at fourteen
news that we'd marry and move far away
promises to stay in touch no matter what
plans in order to change direction

breaking things—
a plate while washing the dishes
the pattern of life to stop the hurt
the silence through persistence and providence
the ice to see what lies ahead

breaking things—
accidentally?
on purpose?
unintentionally
for a reason.

Berry Picking

In Midsummer
Mother dressed me
in long sleeves
long pants
handed me a pail
and said, "Okay, today we're
picking berries.
Follow me."

Uphill all the way
through woods
across the clearing
and there they were—
bushes heavy with fruit
dark plump ripe with sweetness—

One touch and
each berry dropped between my fingers
as the briars caught the back of my hand.

Collecting a few berries in my pail
I asked, "Can I eat some?"
"Yes, you can as long as you fill your pail too."

I spied one slightly larger than the others
touched it
the berry fell
and my hand moved to my mouth.

Mmmm.
Sweet warm juice oozed
across my tongue
down my throat
I was caught by its elixir
bringing satisfaction
until the next and the next and the next
until I could eat no more.

Until Mother said,
"Your pail is not full."
I never picked my fill
Of berries.

Pressing Down Hard
(or, Why Is the Sky Blue?)

Poets speak of the azure sky
and make it seem bluer by the mere repeating of it—
The Azure!
Azure!
Azure!

A child uses a crayon
and presses down hard to make it true
but when she looks up and matches her 'sky blue'
with the real blue sky, the color falls short
as if the Crayola label lied.

She feels cheated and asks her father,
"Daddy, what makes the sky blue?"
"Oh, you'd better go ask your mother,
she taught school, you know."

She finds mother on the porch snapping beans
and the girl asks her then,
"Mom, what makes the sky blue?
Why can't I color it the same?
My box of 64 colors has 'sky blue'
but it doesn't look right!"

Mother pauses,
her hands stopping momentarily as if she's counting
stitches when she's knitting multi-colored yarn into warm
mittens that 'go' with everything.
The green beans stand out against her red apron.

Mother sighs and slowly begins to explain and
the girl is in for a school lesson,
now almost sorry she asked—
Her mother states, 'I suppose that some people believe
the sky's color is the same
everywhere, but I think not!'
She looks up to the sky to muster her memory and then—
"A clear sky is clear azure blue because of the refraction and
decomposition of the sun's light as it travels through the air
and gets more dense and in the color spectrum, blue and violet
refract more easily and spread out more in the sky
as they reflect

off particles floating and—"
Her voice trails off when she realizes the words are too hard for her daughter
and anyway she begins to wonder herself how the yellow sun

could hold blue and give the earth its azure.

The girl is listening no more, having spied a robin's fallen egg.
Picking it up and gently rolling it in her palm,
she takes that moment
to decide for herself what makes the sky blue.
She knows now!
The crayons are all wrong!
Grown-ups are wrong too!
The answer's right there!

A giant robin, far, far away, lost one of its eggs,
falling to the earth and the shell broke
into a million pieces and its color
dissolved in the robin's tears
until heaven was colored
'robin's egg blue'
but because the sky was no longer an egg
someone else named it 'sky blue.'

Poets speak of the color of the sky but
'sky blue' isn't right either, so
to make it true they must repeat
Azure!
Azure!
Azure!

Magic

A friend says that
"magic exists if you're lucky
or open to it" and
he's probably right.

I saw it the other day
when crystal ice
encrusted bare branches
that broke down trees
but brought sparkle
to a bare land
with a presto-change-o
incantation.

I remember it
when the bird's nest
outside my window
produced tiny hungry
beings that eventually
flew after some hesitant
hocus-pocus.

I recall the wand
my daughter
waved while
chanting her
abracadabra
please and thank you—
those magic words
every mother listens for—

knowing that
she did a trick or two
and raised some
magic spells
for future generations.

Dandelions

Primary yellow dandelions
littered the ground with
feathery softness swaying
with the breeze
blowing older
seedy blooms
scattering aloft to
propagate another crop
that overtake tender
wild violets growing
beneath the trees.

The bold weed
shows off and
consumes
precious music
from the Singer
of sad songs
creates magic
from the Artist
of painted words.

I used to love
dandelions as
I learned to blow
the seeds away—
my mistaken
idea of spreading
false beauty
to lure the
unsuspecting heart
into thinking it's
Eternal
only to be
eaten again and again
until no violets remain.

Spring Faith

Each spring after snow melted,
something stirred in the earth.
Something stirred in my brother too.
He started trekking up the hill
sometimes allowing me to follow.
He would point out where the ginseng grew
making a note to return to the spot
to dig some roots he would dry to sell.
He showed me the miracle of wild violets
faithfully facing all Time.

He'd let me pick a few, but they weren't what he really wanted.
Spring meant we'd find wild onions
near rivulets of spring water.
In a good year, we could pull enough
to eat them raw and take the rest to Mom
who cooked them up with fried potatoes for supper.
She hated our reeking breath of wild onions,
but welcomed those precious bulbs and stems
flavoring our life in the spring
faithfully facing all Time.

Sunrise

gold—almost
half way round the sky
magnificence at sunrise

cloud cover comes down
squeezing golden rays
out of the sun

so that clouds take over
glowing with
promise of day.

Transition

I don't need
the equinox
to tell me
spring is here

daffodils trumpet the news

a fat robin sings of spring
on his way north

the young pear tree
planted last year blooms
forth with its first effort
mightily competing with
older ones in the park
that give off a ghostly
show in the night

even you emanate
a sense of your own
transition
as you break from
childhood
into life—
springing forth full of
future yearnings
trying to choose
what's right, what's wrong
and knowing the difference—

the equinox teeters
on a perilous point
and only time tells
where it all ends.

Overturned Life

Tornado warnings
wailed for all to take shelter—
weather forecasters screamed
to get underground or leave!
we fled our home—
birds flew away to safer limbs—
winds whirled through
leaving behind
darkness
broken limbs
pelted rooftops
overturned lives—

Afterward—
in the light of day—
I walked across the yard
picking up odd bits of
broken branches—

I found the nest
upside down in the grass—
and tipping it back with my toe
four naked nestlings fallen—
mouths still open
as if screaming just before
our lives over turned.

Mourning Dove

I watched a dove
on a makeshift nest
two eggs and
her brooding almost at
an end

one egg fell
landed on the ground
with a tiny half-formed dove exposed
all beak and featherless body—

the other egg hatched a healthy
chick fed by the mother with her
"pigeon" milk eagerly taken and
the chick grew fat until
its body flowed over the
nest edge—

one morning I found the lump
of fuzzy feathers lying
still—

the nest now empty
mama dove
nowhere in sight—

from somewhere close by she
cooed in her solitary
mourning.

How It Is

High in the old pear tree,
a cardinal clings to a branch
reaching toward the sky
until he's ready to fly
on to meet his mate
somewhere close by,
giving us a glimpse
of how it is to love
someone.

Autumn Colors

I shuffle my feet
through fallen leaves—

the fragrance of autumn colors
rise making me recall

the hills of gold red orange
mixed with stubborn green—

the last bit of chlorophyll
hanging on a branch—

the tree naps but
awakens from the rustling

as I kick the dried leaves
inhaling autumn colors.

Autumn Meditation

On a still Indian summer day
the sweet smell of autumn
filters through the yellow orange trees
just before the winds
bluster their way into winter
tossing down
drying leaves that
skitter and scatter
along curbs and walls,
crowding around shrubs
as if huddling against
the onslaught of men
hoisting leaf blowers,
their engines droning
out the chatter
warning of
winter's coming.

Eclipse

A partial eclipse of
the moon
turned to full redness
made me think
that something special
was afoot in the sky—

Orion to the east
was lying down on the job
mortally wounded
by the Moon Goddess
foretelling the end of
summer's heat

Sirius
nipped on the heels
of Taurus
after Artemis
sent him to search
for his master
to soothe
her guilt—

Oh, how love
and faithfulness
spur us on
to seek a sense of
stability among the stars
as the full moon
blushes at our folly.

Taking Flight

Each day I watch birds
fly across the yard—
some stop to rest in the old pear tree
some sit on the fence
some cling to the power lines high above.
Today, the wind is strong.
The pear tree is bare now
but the taller oak tries to hold its leaves fast.
I thought I saw a bird skimming the air—
then another
and another.
Then I realized the oak leaves
were taking flight.

Prayer

Bare tree branches
reach up in prayer
asking for reprieve
or forgiveness for
standing leafless
offering no shade
to birds perching
watching for prey
who come too near—
still—serving a purpose—
an answer to prayer.

Snow Falling

Snowflakes fell—
I held out my mittened hands
to catch them—
against the soft darkness
they each stood out—

Specimens of perfection—
crystals of frozen tears
sliced to give cross sections
of life itself
just as Virgil
pointed out
"sunt lacrimae rerum"

tears at the heart of life itself.

Hope—Preface

I spent nearly a month in the hospital when I was 19. I had just given birth to my firstborn, who only survived a day and a half. It was a strange time and even stranger to be in the hospital during a period of what most would think of as grieving; yet, there was so much happening around me that I am not sure I grieved in any way that most would define it as such. I was in a military hospital in Tachikawa, Japan, a hospital that served as the major staging site for the severely wounded coming out of Vietnam. If they survived the battlefield but needed more treatment than could be handled by the MASH units, the wounded soldiers were airlifted to Tachikawa. Some healed and were either sent back into combat in Vietnam or sent home, depending on their injuries. Others were cared for until they were well enough to be airlifted to a hospital in the States. Some were airlifted in coffins, landing first at Travis AFB in California and then sent on to either their hometown or to a military cemetery. Vietnam and the war that raged there left a strange pall over many lives—people who are now in their sixties know what I mean, especially those who experienced some part of it firsthand.

Hope

Never knew his name
but we got to know him,
as nurses pushed the gurney
up and down the hallway
every other day.

We'd see him go by in the morning—
return in the afternoon
just before our dinner meals arrived
up and down the hallway.

Up and down the hallway,
he rode, lying very still on the special gurney,
seldom looking left or right,
so he didn't notice our stares
up and down the hallway.

The nurse said he had dialysis—
his kidneys didn't work—
one day I asked why
he stopped
going up and down the hallway.

The nurse said he didn't make it—
the bouncing betty had blown off
the bottom half—
it remained in Vietnam.
He left us but
I still see him going

up and down the hallway—
hoping.

Armistice, 1918

Birds watched as men moved
forward
across pitted fields bordered by wire
through bared trees standing sentry
as the big guns still fired;
the hour struck—
one last gun sounded far away—
then silence.
Armistice began.
The birds sighed
then piped to the world—
"Peace at last!"

Motorbiking in Wales

To mount your bike
I step up on the pillion
swing my leg over the back
and alight on the seat—
sliding into you.
I wrap my arms around your waist—
You instruct me to look over
your shoulder when we go 'round curves
so my head bobs from side to side—
the roads in Wales have lots of curves—

We speed out of Harlech along
the coast to Dolgellau
where we stop for coffee and talk.
Then to Bala for a lunch of
fish and chips and mushy peas.
From there the bike climbs and heads
us along Lake Celyn—
once a long valley
now flooded to give water to
the English in Liverpool but
inflamed national pride too—
I can't blame the Welsh.

Trees guard the banks and
flowers bloom pink, yellow, purple, blue
with a sweet fragrance in the air as
we speed by some unseen shrub
then gone too soon.
When we stop to read a plaque
and you step behind a tree to pee,
I wait near the bike trying
to recollect the fragrance
to ask you but I can't describe it
so I just remount the bike
and hold on to you.

Now—
I wait and recall
our afternoon—
holding on—

my arms wrapped round your waist—

to a memory
I can't fully describe.

One Evening in Budapest

One evening in Budapest
holding lit candles
we hooked fingers to form circles
and we did the shepherd's dance
and we were one.

One evening in Budapest
a poem was spoken in Hungarian
with no English translation
but the poem was full of soul
and we were one.

One evening in Budapest
a lady's fingers flew over piano keys
and played Liszt and Bartok
until she slowed to stillness
and we were one.

One evening in Budapest
a Japanese soprano sang
a flawless aria from
Madame Butterfly and almost cried
and we were one.

One evening in Budapest
we watched a mime watching us
as he opened invisible doors
and we laughed when he became a babushka
and we were one.

One evening in Budapest
someone else played piano
an improvised flamenco that
made us want to dance
and we were one.

One evening in Budapest
a techno theater dance troupe
stirred us with their sensuous bodies
moving to the strong music's beat
and we were one.

One evening in Budapest
a band of flutes and drums
sitars and rain sticks and didgeridoos

created harmony from cacophony
and we were one.

One evening in Budapest
we were many from other
parts of the world
we felt kinship
we felt peace
we were one
because of
one evening
in Budapest.

Finding Shoes

In the restroom—there—
near the last stall—
a pair of navy blue heels—
slightly scuffed
sweat stained with wear
a cheap pink bow to decorate
the top of the toe
and matches the pink lining—
no one is around to claim them

I wonder who
left them behind.

perchance she was in a hurry to change
into jeans and boots
or maybe she was just swept off her feet
and out the door for the weekend—
or perhaps she
entered the stall
stepped out of her shoes
so she could slink away
barefooted
making no sound
as she escaped toward
freedom from a past that
demanded she wear navy blue heels
to match her navy blue suit
with a pink fabric flower
saying 'yes, ma'am'
and 'no, ma'am'
as she tried to please everyone
but pleasing no one—
except the cleaning woman

who picks up those navy blue shoes
and says "those are just what my girl needs
to go with her little navy suit
with the pink flower pinned to her chest!"
no one's the wiser
and I don't tell
as she carries the shoes away
in her cleaning cart.

Moonlight Sonata

"Moonlight Sonata" after a dinner
of talking teaching and how it used
to be—wishing
for better days ahead
and behind—
more moonlight and
poetry—
that's what we need—
more sonata and less
sonorous pronouncements from
our leaders who know
so little of our lives
and what we really want—
more music to make
our lives bearable through
the sublime night—
listening to the struggling notes
to make the world
a bit more
beautiful.

Your World
for Donna

You give me
your views of the world—

through each
landscape
including the
windmills that churn
the air and add
power across the
hills—

through each
rose and peony
daffodil and violet
those colors of
every season
of your life—

through each
photo of your
family as the
grandkids grow
before your eyes—

through your
camera lens
you give me the world
as you know it.

Making the Grade

On that first day of class
your talk was full of excitement
reflected in your eyes
as you looked forward to learning
and making the grade—
Today I missed you—
again—from class—
and wondered where
you'd gone—
Then late in the day
you loomed in my office door—
wearing camouflage and
holding your fatigue cap
and apologizing
that you would have to withdraw—
"Nothing against you or the course
It's just that . . . that my unit's
been called up and
I'll be shipping out"—
Gone was that boyish grin—
Absent was your yearning—
And instead your eyes
Told the truth of your fear—
And all I could do was reassure you
With "Take care" and
"Let me know if you ever need any help—
after you come home."
I hope you made the grade.

Joy of Giving

On the far edge of winter
looking toward spring
I gave my friend
a shell in a heart-shaped box.

Someone told me once,
"Tis the sender's choice to give.
How could I not like something
intended to give joy and by giving,
thereby getting some for thyself?"

Oh, to give more from the heart
and less from the edge of winter
looking backward.

Bertha Wise is a retired Professor of English at Oklahoma City Community College. She earned a BS in English Education and MA in English from the University of Central Oklahoma (UC0). Originally from central New York State, she found her way to Oklahoma over thirty years ago through a circuitous route, having also lived in such diverse locations as Arizona, New Hampshire, California, and South Carolina in the U.S. and Tachikawa, Japan. Bertha's many travels have informed her poetry, but most of all, she finds inspiration from the memories made along the way. Several of her poems have been published in various college and university literary journals including Baraza (at UCO), Redbud (at OSU-OKC), Pegasus (at Rose State College), Absolute (at OCCC) and Dragon Poet Review. Two cats named Roscoe and Cato currently live with Bertha and her husband Guy Herrick in Oklahoma.

www.ingramcontent.com/pod-product-compliance
Lightning Source LLC
Chambersburg PA
CBHW030202100526
44592CB00009B/407